A Social Story™
for the Rest of Us

For 30 years, parents and professionals have been writing Social Stories for those with autism. Here's one for the rest of us!

Carol Gray

Foreword by Dr. Siobhan Timmins, MB.BS. (London)

A Social Story™ for the Rest of Us

All marketing and publishing rights guaranteed to and reserved by:

FUTURE HORIZONS INC.

(800) 489-0727

(817) 277-0727

(817) 277-2270 (fax)

E-mail: info@FHautism.com

www.FHautism.com

ISBN: 978-1-949177-51-0

In awe and appreciation of my student, Eric,
whose comments launched the
first Social Story and all that followed.

Preface

Autism is a lifelong opportunity to discover that which should have been obvious in the first place. Take confusion and anxiety, for example. Most of the first Social Stories™ describe new or unfamiliar events, like a field trip, or the rationale behind the statements, requests, and behaviors of others. I was often surprised at how the Stories seemed to immediately erase student apprehension and replace it with a more confident and effective response to a situation or event. Initially intrigued at how well (and fast!) Social Stories worked for my students, the real shock came years later when I realized how the Stories were changing me—admittedly, at a much slower pace! Gathering information and writing in the accurate and unshakably sincere Social Story format revealed the errors in my interpretation and attribution of student behavior. This process gradually reframed how I think, and that, in turn, changed everything. The positive storm of autism, anxiety, and Social Stories replaced my professional self-doubts with a new understanding of the goal. *A Social Story for the Rest of Us* is a summary of what I have learned to date.

In the mid-1970s, I began my teaching career at Pinewood Elementary School in Jenison, Michigan with four students who were diagnosed with severe autism. Life in general, and specifically the understanding of autism, was dramatically different than it is today. There were few resources available; I had one book about autism on my classroom shelf. Communication with the parents of my students was reliant on landline telephones and handwritten notes. I was lonely at work. I didn't have any colleagues to speak of, no teacher down the hall to share experiences or ideas.

I kept a professional journal. It was a place to replay my frustrations. The phrase, "this is my last year" appears many times. It's a theme that runs cover to cover. Knowing that I could exit in June made it possible for me to return every September. In a way, I started working on this Story in that professional diary.

In 2003, I was contacted by Samantha, a high school student, with a request for a written interview as part of her senior project. I retrieved my journal from an old box. Time has a way of sanding off the rough edges of our past mistakes. My journal didn't allow me that luxury; it held the unforgiving details of my self-recorded history. Samantha's questions led to a discussion of professional confusion. I shared one of my earliest journal entries with her, describing the internal tug-of-war between uncertainty and discovery:

> Sometimes I look around my classroom and I don't know what I am seeing. I can describe only how it looks. I am so used to understanding what I see. That isn't possible here. More puzzling is to wonder what each child is seeing, perhaps seeing the same thing but perceiving it differently? I become disheartened when I talk myself into believing that I will never know the world that the children know and that they will never know mine. It's a destructive way for a teacher to think, so I never let myself dwell on that for too long. Not for too long, but it crosses my mind often (Gray, 1976; as cited in Gray, 2003).

Twenty years later, and six years after the discovery of Social Stories, parent and professional uncertainty in educational programming for children diagnosed with autism was still an issue. I saw it as a threat to our efforts:

> Confusion is uncomfortable for us. People like to know what to do. Knowing what to do is reassuring. It makes us feel competent and in control. At the same time, it leaves us vulnerable to a "McFix" approach—it doesn't have to be a good solution; it just has to be presented with that implication.

> We are at risk for fast and ineffective interventions. Adding to the confusion are other people who share their convictions (assumptions that have gone absolute) regarding why a specific behavior occurs, without taking the opportunity to be confused. It is common for us to believe that doing is equal to knowing what to do. This is not always true (Gray, 1997, p. 18).

A federal Challenge Grant (1986-1991, contract #86300) made it possible to place our students in a series of vocational experiences in the community, with instructional assistants as coaches. During this time, our awareness of the contributions of parents and professionals to the social impairment "in autism" grew, along with our social humility.

> Ben, a severely impaired nonverbal student with autism, was in training in the upholstery department of a furniture manufacturer, learning to sweep up fabric scraps. Ben could perform the

task within a small area but required prompts to identify and move to new sections that required sweeping.

Ben's teacher and coach had an idea. They placed large plastic fabric arrows on the floor to direct Ben to the next area. He learned to pick up each arrow and put it in a special pocket on his supply cart before moving on. The idea worked well for several training sessions.

One day, instead of placing the arrows in the pocket, Ben threw them into the trash one-by-one as he completed sweeping each section. The coach could have assumed that Ben's behavior was oppositional. Instead, she decided that he may be telling her that he no longer needed the arrows. The coach left the arrows in the trash, and the student worked successfully in the following weeks without them (Gray, 1992, paraphrased).

Autism co-authors every Social Story that I write. It's been a patient writing partner, contributing to each Story for over two decades while the much-needed *A Social Story for the Rest of Us* remained unaddressed. As I mentioned, I am a slower study of Social Stories than my students. I began gathering information for the following Story on my first day of teaching in late August of 1976, and continued in that effort for over four decades until October of 2019. With autism as a focused co-author, *A Social Story for the Rest of Us* was completed within a few days.

References

Gray, C. (2003). Answers for Samantha. Personal correspondence. Retrieved from https://carolgraysocialstories.com/wp-content/uploads/2015/10/Answers-for-Samantha.pdf

Gray, C. (1997). Gray's guide to neurotypical behavior: Appreciating the challenge that we present to people with autistic spectrum disorders. Part II: Understanding the social impairment in neurotypical. *The Morning News,* Summer 1997, 16-20. Jenison, MI: Jenison Public Schools. Retrieved from https://carolgraysocialstories.com/articles-newsletters/the-morning-newsjenison-autism-journal/

Gray, C. (1992). The curriculum system: Success as an educational outcome. Jenison, MI: Jenison Public Schools. Retrieved from https://carolgraysocialstories.com/wp-content/uploads/2015/10/Here.-The-Curriculum-System.pdf

Gray, C. (1976). Professional journal, unpublished.

Foreword

In 1997, I sat in the audience of a conference on autism, as both a parent and professional, eager for new information that would help me understand my son. I listened as Carol Gray described the different, yet equally valid, perspective of a child with autism. She explained how this difference deserves our utmost respect; it requires us to abandon all of our neurotypical assumptions and interpretations as we look at situations in which our children need help. Carol explained how Social Stories™ share information and improve mutual understanding. We understand the child better, and the child understands us better. It's a two-way process that benefits both sides.

I left the conference transformed. Enlightened, inspired, and brimming with hope, I began to plot a course my child and I could follow to navigate the social seas together using Social Stories and the Social Story philosophy as waypoints. Amazing things happened as a result: all our communication and interactions became more meaningful, effective, and joyful, and my son began (and continues) to thrive.

Carol has since become my mentor, my colleague, and good friend—as well as my heroine! I was thrilled and honored when she asked me to write a foreword to this book. I believe this Social Story encapsulates everything I heard in her first presentation nearly thirty years ago, and all neurotypicals need to absorb it.

Social Stories share the neurotypical perspective with children and adults with autism, so it makes sense that we have this Story explain the perspective of people with autism to neurotypicals. *A Social Story for the Rest of Us* is a little book with a big heart and an important message. Carol has brilliantly pulled together what she has learned as an outstanding autism teacher and world-leading autism consultant. She describes how every person with autism is "unique twice": once as a human being, and again as a person with autism. This is a Story that our children with autism want us to read, remember, and implement as we work with them.

A Social Story™ for the Rest of Us

I have returned to listen to Carol present again and again to reinvigorate, refresh and "reset" my social curiosity. I will use this Story in the same way, and frame it on my wall as a daily visual reminder. It is a pleasure to encourage everyone to do the same!

— Siobhan Timmins, MB.BS. (London)

author of

Successful Social Stories™ for Young Children with Autism: Growing Up with Social Stories™ (2016)

Successful Social Stories™ for School and College Students with Autism: Growing Up with Social Stories™ (2017)

Developing Resilience in Young People with Autism using Social Stories™: Growing Up With Social Stories™ (2017)

Successful Social Articles into Adulthood: Growing Up with Social Stories™: Growing up with Social Stories™ (2018)

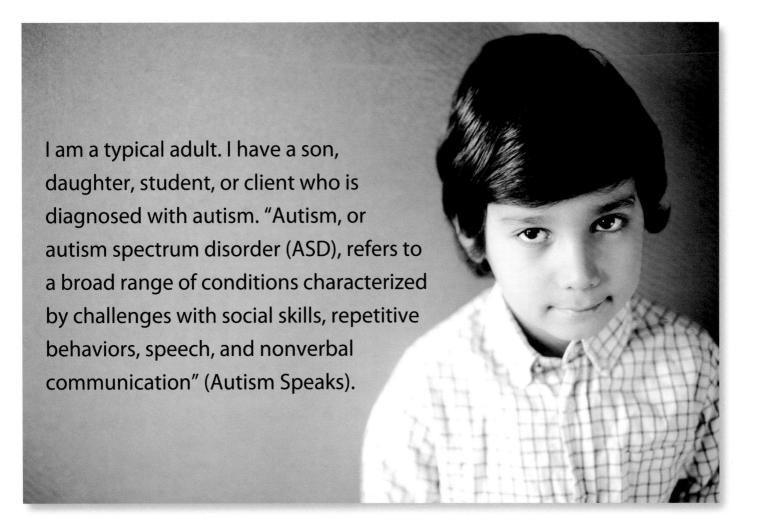

I am a typical adult. I have a son, daughter, student, or client who is diagnosed with autism. "Autism, or autism spectrum disorder (ASD), refers to a broad range of conditions characterized by challenges with social skills, repetitive behaviors, speech, and nonverbal communication" (Autism Speaks).

Dr. Stephen Shore, a professor at Adelphi University and a person with autism, has said that "if you've met one person with autism, you've met one person with autism."

This means that I will need to learn about autism over and over again, as long as I keep meeting people with autism. This is okay.

Every person is the result of a combination of genes and life experiences. Together, they express themselves in a one-time-only physical appearance and a never-to-be-repeated constellation of strengths, weaknesses, temperament, personality, and talent.

Despite that, most "typical" people perceive and respond to sights, sounds, and social factors within a similar or "typical" range. As they grow, they begin making assumptions about what other people know, think, feel, or believe and pride themselves in how often they are right. I will try to abandon thinking I am right about this sort of thing all the time.

Just like everyone else, a child, adolescent, or adult with autism is unique. In a way, having autism is like being unique twice—once as a person, and again because of autism.

For people with autism, the perception and interpretation of sights, sounds, and social factors are atypical at times. When I'm with a person with autism, I will try to recognize all that we have in common, respect our differences, and respond accordingly.

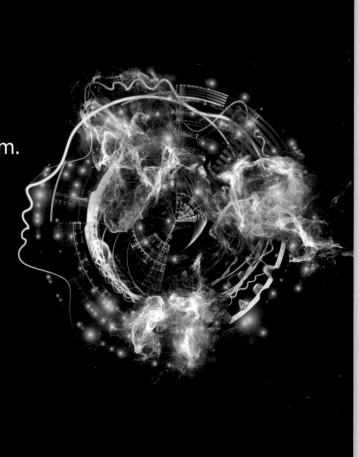

Adults often try to explain the "atypical" responses of a child with autism by citing "typical" motivations; though they are likely to be in error. People with autism are more at ease with people who are socially curious, who take time to gather information about how things look, sound, and feel to another person.

Social curiosity comes naturally to some people; others learn it with practice. A few people are "socially decided" and do not entertain the possibility of human experiences outside of their own. I will try to be socially curious.

A sense of humor is essential when working with a child, adolescent, or adult with autism. Humor renews energy, resets focus, and sustains the socially curious when they are confused.

It is theorized that curious people make fewer social errors and are more likely to recognize and fix the mistakes that they do make. I will try to process my mistakes with creativity and a forgiving sense of humor.

To successfully raise, teach, or consult on behalf of an individual with autism is to ensure equal access to information. People with autism may be misled by anything, animate or inanimate: nonverbal social factors, a single word in a conversation, a billboard along the highway. I will try to watch out for this and be ready to describe or explain things.

Whether I am a parent, teacher, therapist, or physician, I am part of an educational team. The best educational teams recognize that:

- Feeling safe facilitates learning.

- Understanding what's next reduces anxiety.

- Personalized structure builds predictability, supports effort, and builds confidence.

- Successful communication occurs when meaning is unaltered as it travels from sender to recipient and back again.

- Autism can alter intended meaning.

- Using autism-friendly phrasing and formats helps to ensure that intended messages remain intact.

- Social concepts can be taught.

- Being social is often fun, and best taught in a positive and enjoyable way.

- Social concepts make it possible for social skills to internalize and cross boundaries.

- People are usually employed doing something that they have done well all along.

- What adults say and do, and how they say and do it, matters. A lot. I will try to be an effective member of an educational team.

I am ready to learn about autism repeatedly. Each person is unique, and autism is never the same twice. Social curiosity complements autism. Humor re-energizes patience and re-sets attention and focus. Children, adolescents, and adults with autism sometimes need educators to structure and ensure their equal access to information. Everything that I say and do on behalf of a person with autism has an impact. Positive and creative teaching fosters growth.

My name is _____ and this my Social Story.
I will keep it in a safe place, just in case I want to read it again sometime
or share it with someone else.

References

Autism Speaks. What is autism? Retrieved online from Autism Speaks: *https://www.autismspeaks.org/what-autism*

Rosenfeld, J. (April 11, 2018, updated March 27, 2019). 11 scientific benefits of having a laugh. Retrieved online from Mental Floss: *https://mentalfloss.com/article/539632/scientific-benefits-having-laugh*

Shore, S. What is autism? Retrieved online from Autism Speaks: *https://www.autismspeaks.org/what-autism*